TREASURY OF LITERATURE

WRITER'S JOURNAL

HOLD ON TIGHT

Grateful acknowledgment is made to Marian Reiner, on behalf of Sandra Liatsos, for permission to reprint "Night" by Sandra Liatsos. Text copyright © 1989 by Sandra Liatsos.

Printed in the United States of America

ISBN 0-15-301269-2
1 2 3 4 5 6 7 8 9 10   030   97   96   95   94

HARCOURT BRACE & COMPANY

Orlando   Atlanta   Austin   Boston   San Francisco   Chicago   Dallas   New York
Toronto   London

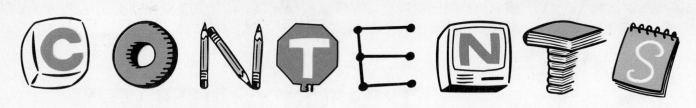

CONTENTS

IN·THE·NIGHT

3–4

ON·OUR·WAY

20–21

I CAN'T SLEEP

PEACE AT LAST
Let Mr. Bear Sleep **5**
Bear Town News **6**

SLEEPYTIME POEMS
A Night Poem **7**

DREAMS
I Live Here **8**
Mouse and his Friends **9**

SHADOW PICTURES
Duck Talk **10**

STARRY NIGHT

STARS
My Trip to the Stars **11**
All About My Chart **12**

SLEEPING OUTDOORS
My Night Outdoors **13**

IN MY ROOM

THERE'S AN ALLIGATOR UNDER MY BED
Under My Bed **14–15**
Detective Notes **16–17**

making your own **magazine 18–19**

SIGNS OF SPRING

HENRY AND MUDGE IN PUDDLE TROUBLE
What Will I Do? **22**

TOMMY
What Tommy's Plant Said **23**

LITTLE SEEDS
How to Grow Silly Garden Plants **24**

ALL ABOUT SEEDS
All About… **25**

SILLY JOURNEYS

HENNY PENNY
Henny Penny Herald **26**

ANIMALS ON THE MOVE
My Jokes **27**

LOST AND FOUND

LOST!
I Help the Bear Write a Letter **28**
I Know Why the Girl Is Happy **29**

OH WHERE, OH WHERE HAS MY LITTLE DOG GONE?
I Help Find a Lost Dog **30**

JAMAICA'S FIND
What Edgar Dog Said **31**

making your own **magazine 32–33**

Acknowledgments **34**

Writer's Handbook **35–38**

YOUR OWN MAGAZINE **39–48**

BOOK FIVE · IN·THE·NIGHT

Read the poem.
Then turn to page 4.

NIGHT

Night is a blanket
that covers the small
squirrels and chipmunks
and covers the tall
horses out sleeping
under the tree.
I like the night.
It's a blanket for me.

Sandra Liatsos

(your name)

Likes the Night

☞ Have children write what they like about the night. Have them draw a picture to go with their writing.

Do Not Disturb

Let Mr. Bear Sleep

by _____
(your name)

☞ Ask children to imagine that Mr. Bear is taking a nap to catch up on his lost sleep. Explain that he is going to hang this sign outside his door to be sure he is not disturbed. Have children write Mr. Bear's message on the Do Not Disturb sign.

Bear Town News

Bear Town News since 1902

Wednesday

Details

Main Idea

by _____ (your name)

☞ Have children write an article for the Bear Town News. Have them examine the picture and write the main idea as a headline. Then have them write the details about the picture.

A NIGHT POEM

BY _____
(your name)

1 Write the names of two things found in the night sky.

Night
_____
_____

2 Write the names of two nighttime animals.

_____
_____

3 Write one word that tells about a night sound.

_____
Night

☞ Invite children to write a five-word poem about the night. Tell them to begin each word with a capital letter. Have children read their poems aloud.

Lives Here

(your name)

Have children draw themselves on the left. Then have them write a conversation that might take place between themselves and the girl on the right.

Mouse and his Friends

by _____
(your name)

☞ Have children write about what is
happening in the picture. Tell them to
include as many details as they can.

Duck Talk

by _____
(your name)

☞ Ask children to imagine that the duck shadow can talk. Have them write what the duck shadow might say to the rabbit shadow.

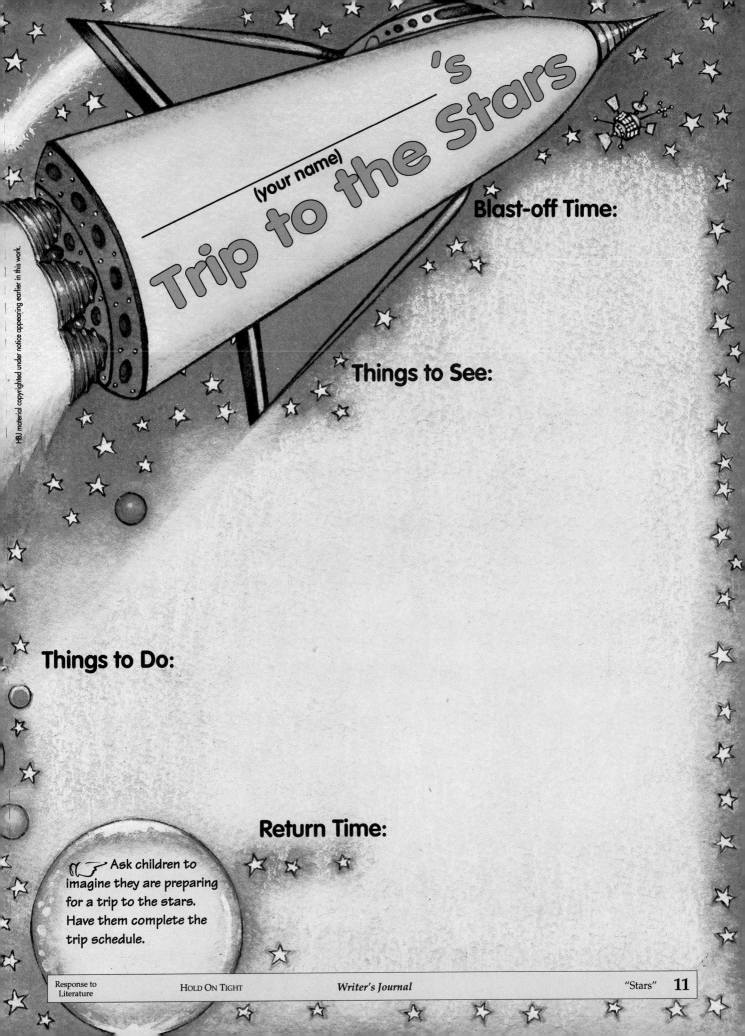

_____'s
(your name)

Trip to the Stars

Blast-off Time:

Things to See:

Things to Do:

Return Time:

✍ Ask children to imagine they are preparing for a trip to the stars. Have them complete the trip schedule.

Stars			
Airplanes			
Owls			

All About _____'s Chart

(your name)

Have children count the stars in the sky and draw an X on the chart to represent each one. Have them do the same with the airplane and owls. Then have children write about the information on their chart. Encourage them to use the word <u>more</u> when they write.

_____'s **Night Outdoors**

(your name)

☞ Ask children to imagine that they are on a camping trip. Have them draw themselves in the tent. Then have children write about their experience sleeping outdoors.

Under

_____'s

(your name)

Bed

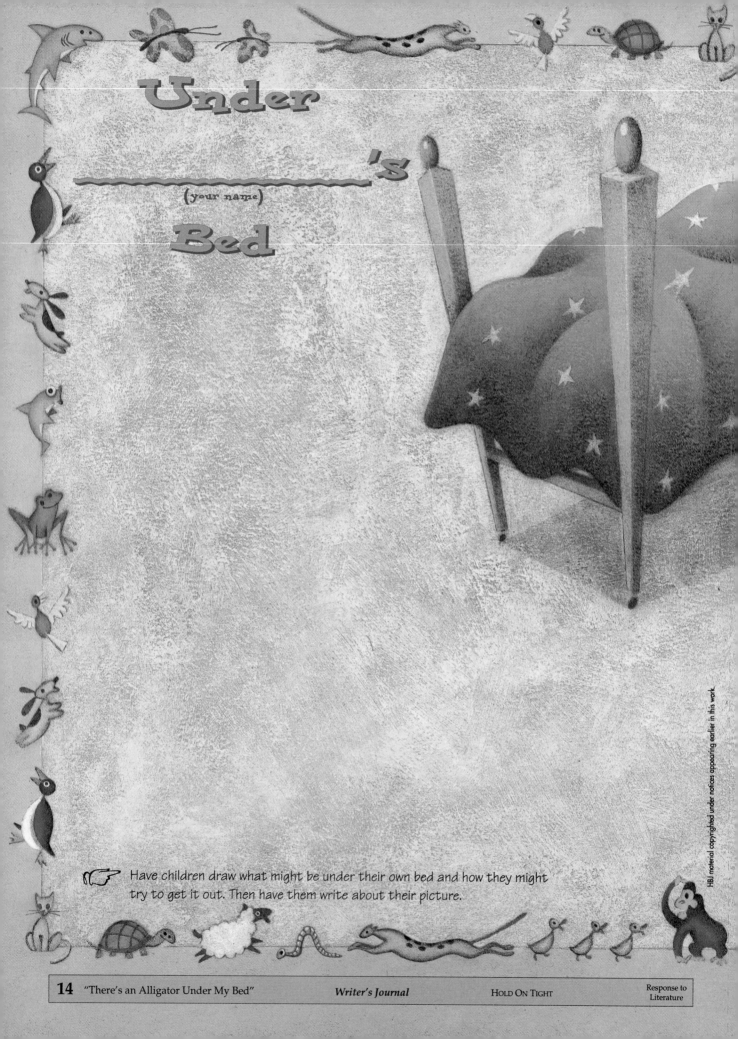

👉 Have children draw what might be under their own bed and how they might try to get it out. Then have them write about their picture.

Detective _____'s
(your name)

Notes

Who? _____

_____

What? _____

_____

Where? _____

_____

When? _____

☞ Ask children to imagine that they are detectives.
Have them look for important details in the picture.
Have children answer the questions *who?*, *what?*,
where?, and *when?* on their detective notepad.

MAKING YOUR

1 Starting Your Magazine

Turn to pages 39 and 40. Read these pages to find out more about your magazine.

2 MAKING A COVER

Turn to page 41. Make the front cover of your magazine.

Go to page 41 to make your cover.

3 Making the Editor-in-Chief page

You are the Editor-in-Chief! Turn to page 43 in your magazine. You will tell about yourself on this page.

Cut out magazine pictures of things you like.

Draw things you like to do.

Ideas for telling about yourself

Draw a picture of yourself.

Write about your pictures.

Go to page 43 to publish your Editor-in-Chief.

OWN MAGAZINE

4 WRITING YOUR SPECIAL STORY

BEGINNING

Think of a special time you have had. Your special time will make a good story. Draw a little picture to show how your story begins.

MIDDLE

Think again about your special time. Draw a little picture to show what happens next.

ENDING

How does your story end? Draw a picture. Tell your story to a classmate.

Go to pages 44, 45, and 46 to publish your special story.

BOOK ON·OUR·WAY FIVE

Read or sing this song.
Then turn to page 21.

ANIMAL RIDDLES

The bear went over the mountain,

The bear went over the mountain,

The bear went over the mountain,

To see what he could see.

To see what he could see,

To see what he could see,

The bear went over the mountain

To see what he could see.

On_____'s Way
(your name)

☞ Have children draw their face in the Me sign and trace a line down the path on which they'd like to travel. Have children write about what they would see on their way.

Let It Grow.

Pick It!

What will _____ do?
(your name)

Tell children that it is their turn to decide what to do with the snow glory. Ask them whether they will let it grow or pick it. Have children write about their decision.

What Tommy's Plant Said

by _____
(your name)

☞ Ask children to imagine that Tommy's plant could talk. Have them write what the plant might say.

How to Grow Silly Garden Plants

by _____ (your name)

Have children identify the silly garden plants. Then ask them to draw some of their own. Have them write how to plant and care for their silly garden plants.

All About

by _____

(your name)

☞ Ask children to write their own nonfiction article. Have them draw a picture to go with their writing.

Henny Penny Herald

Monday

The Sky is Falling!

by _____ (Your Name)

What Happened?

What Shall We Do?

Have children write a newspaper article for the Henny Penny Herald about the sky falling.

_____'s Jokes
(your name)

Teacher: What did the zebra say to the horse?

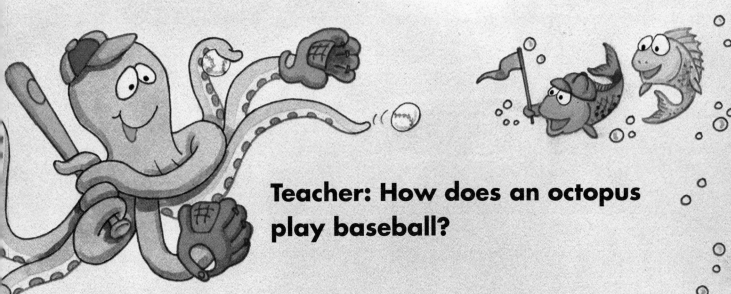

Teacher: How does an octopus play baseball?

☞ Have children write the punch line for each joke. Remind them that there is no correct or incorrect response. Invite children to share their jokes with a partner.

_____
(your name)

Helps the Bear Write a Letter

Dear Friend,

Your friend,
Bear

☞ Ask children to imagine they are helping
the bear from "Lost" write a thank-you
note to the boy. Have them write what the
bear might say in his letter.

 HBJ material copyrighted under notices appearing earlier in this work.

_____ **Knows Why**
(your name) **the Girl is Happy**

Have children write their conclusions about why the girl is happy.

_____ (your name) **Helps Find a Lost Dog**

 Have children draw a lost dog in the picture. Then have them draw a line leading the woman to her dog. Ask children to write about what happens along the way.

What Edgar Dog Said

by _____

(your name)

☞ Ask children to write what Edgar
the stuffed dog might say to
Jamaica, if he could talk.

MAKING YOUR

1 Sharing Information

You know about many things. There is one page in your magazine for writing your information. Read page 47.

What do you know a lot about? What information can you share? Finish this sentence:

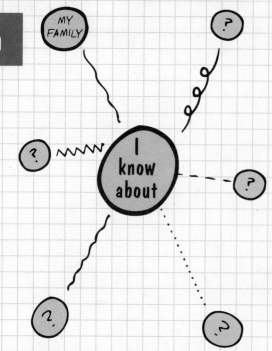

I Know About _____

2 Sharing and Learning with a Friend

What do you know a lot about?
Draw a picture of it in the box.
Tell a classmate all about your picture.
Share your information. Now listen as
your classmate shares information.

OWN MAGAZINE

3 PUTTING YOUR IDEAS TOGETHER

3 What information did you share with your classmate? What information will you share in your magazine? Draw three pictures. Have each picture show information that you want to share in your magazine.

Go to page 47 to publish your information.

4 FINISHING UP YOUR MAGAZINE

4 Your magazine is almost finished. You have two things to do:

Finish Your Table of Contents

Write titles for your story and your information. Your teacher will help you.

Make Your Back Cover

Draw pictures. Cut out pictures. Make a colorful back cover.

Go to page 48 to make your back cover.

ACKNOWLEDGMENTS

Text Selections

Grateful acknowledgment is made to Marian Reiner, on behalf of Sandra Liatsos, for permission to reprint "Night" by Sandra Liatsos. Text copyright © 1989 by Sandra Liatsos.

Illustration Credits

Bernard Adnet 2; Shirley Beckes 16, 31; Mark Corcoran 11; Laura Cornell 22, 23; Janice Edelman 2, 18–19, 32–33, 34; Kim Wilson Eversz 7, 17; Tuko Fujisaki 4; Fred Harsh 6; Robbie Marantz 24; Shelley Matheis 5, 8; Scott Matthews 2, 18–19, 32–33, 34; Susan Miller 12; Michael Moran 10, 13, 25, 29; Judith Pfeiffer 26, 28; Evan Polenghi 9; Brian Schatell 14, 15, 30; Rochelle Valdivia 21, 27; Don Weller 2; **Unit Opener Art:** Bernard Adnet 3; Tina Davis 3, 20; Don Weller 20

 Robert Dale, Bernard Adnet, Stacey May, Janice Edelman 35-38

Scott Matthews, Janice Edelman 39-48

WRITER'S HANDBOOK

This is your Writer's Handbook. It will help you revise and proofread your Magazine. You can use it to check your other writing, too.

END MARKS

Every sentence ends with an end mark.

Use a **period** at the end of a sentence that tells something.

> A star glows hot.

Use a **question mark** at the end of a sentence that asks something.

> Are all the stars as hot as our sun?

Use an **exclamation point** at the end of a sentence that shows strong feeling.

> Some are even hotter!

CAPITAL LETTERS

Begin the **first word** of a sentence with a capital letter.

Do you know how seeds are planted? **Sometimes** they just fall to the ground.

Write the **word** I as a capital letter.

I climbed in to have a nap, and when I woke up, I was lost!

ME!

Begin the **name of a person** with a capital letter.

Jamaica was almost as happy as **Kristin**.

People

Begin the **title of a person** with a capital letter. These are titles:

Mr. Mrs.
Ms. Miss
Dr.

"Oh, no!" said **Mr.** Bear.

Titles of a Person

Other Capital Letters

Begin the **name of a pet** with a capital letter.

> Every day he stood with **Mudge** and looked at the flower.

Animal Names

Begin the **name of a day of the week** with a capital letter.

> Did Jamaica go to the park on **Tuesday**?

Saturday July 4 Independence Day

Begin the **name of a month** with a capital letter.

> Did Henry find the snow glory in **June**?

Month

Begin each important word in the **title of a story** with a capital letter.

> **"Peace at Last"** is a funny story. After we read **"Stars,"** we went out to see the sky at night.

Titles

EDITOR'S MARKS

You can use these marks when you revise and proofread your own writing.

≡ Make this a capital letter.
⊙ Add a period.
? Add a question mark.
! Add an exclamation point.

My dad and i like to look at the moon⊙ Sometimes we see the moon in the afternoon. sometimes we even see it in the morning! i like the moon best when it is big and bright⊙ when do you like to look at the moon?

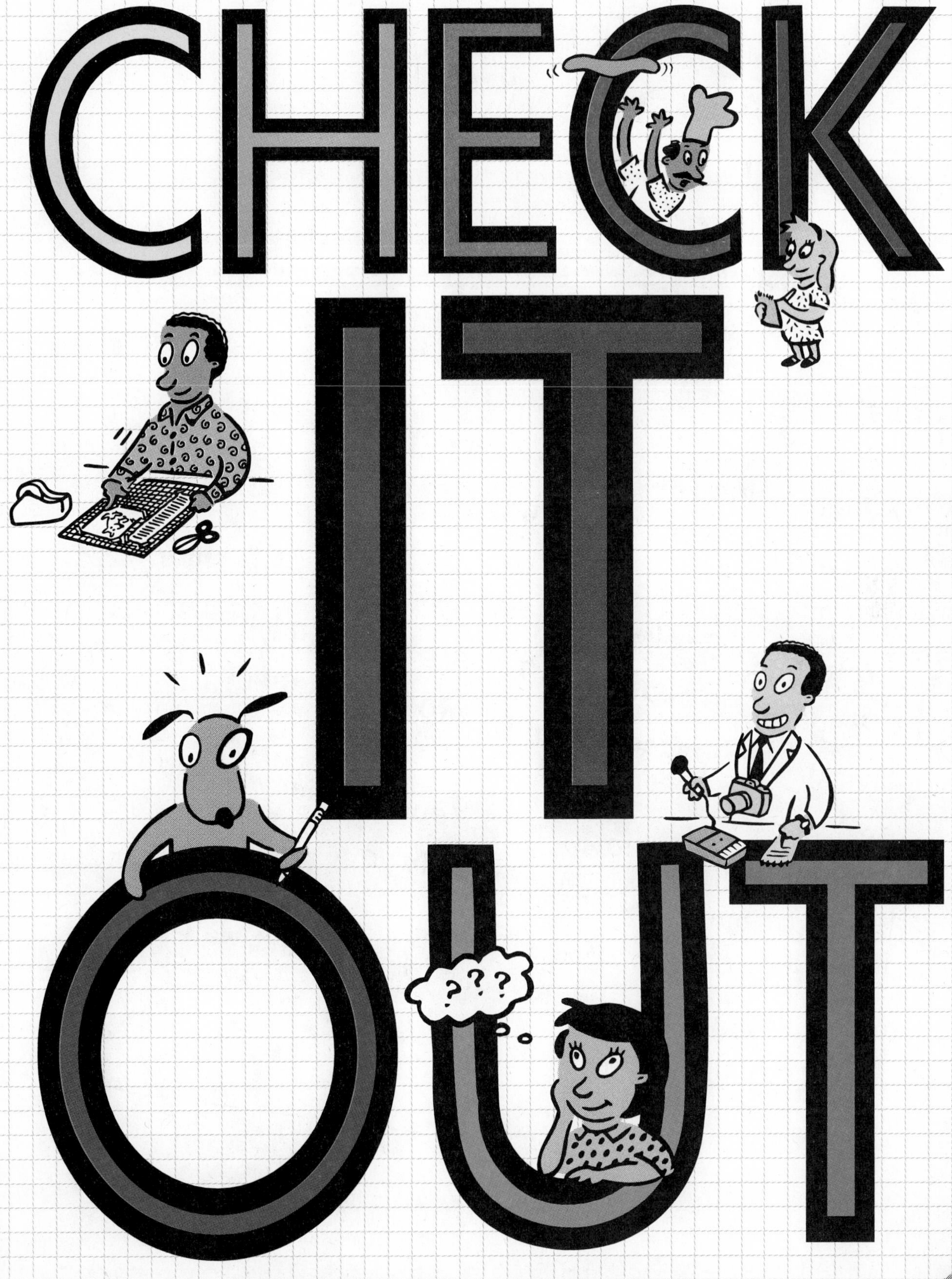
CHECK
IT
OUT
???

Dear Editor-in-Chief,

That's you!

You are going to make your very own magazine. You are the boss. You write the stories.

Your magazine is very special. Why? Because this magazine is about you. You are going to turn the next eight pages into your own special magazine.

You will have a lot of help. Your teacher will help you. Your classmates will help you.

Are you ready, boss? Your friends can't wait to read your magazine.

☞ This magazine project is a collaborative classroom effort. Children will write, illustrate, cut, paste, and publish three writing projects. In addition, the children will design their magazine covers and complete their table of contents. Please read each magazine page to the class and guide children through each project.

_____'s **magazine**

(your name)

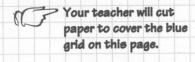 Your teacher will cut
paper to cover the blue
grid on this page.

Your cover

Make your cover!

▸ Cut out pictures.
Draw pictures. Make
a picture cover that
tells about you.
▸ Paste your pictures
on the cut paper.
▸ Paste the cut
paper on top of the
blue grid.
▸ Write your name in
your favorite color.

EQUIPMENT

paper

pencils,
markers

scissors

COVER

paste

old magazines
or newspapers

contents

MEET THE EDITOR-IN-CHIEF!

· **3**

(Write your name on this line.)

MY SPECIAL STORY

· **4**

(Write your story's title here.)

SHARING INFORMATION

· **7**

(Write your title here.)

_____ **is the**

editor-in-chief.

3

 Your teacher will cut paper to cover the blue grid on this page.

Meet the editor-in-chief!

Draw! Write! Paste!

▸ Draw pictures. Cut out pictures. Use pictures that tell about you. Use pictures that tell about something you like.

▸ Write a sentence under each picture.

▸ Paste your pictures and sentences on the cut paper.

▸ Paste the cut paper on top of the blue grid.

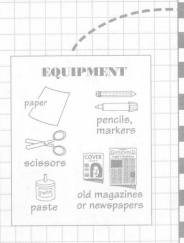

EQUIPMENT

paper

pencils, markers

scissors

paste

old magazines or newspapers

_____ **has a**
(your name)

special story.

 Your teacher will cut paper to cover the blue grids on this page and on the next two pages.

My special story

Draw! Write! Paste!

▸ Think of a story.
▸ Draw pictures for your story on the pieces of cut paper.
▸ Write a sentence for each picture.
▸ Write the name of your story.
▸ Paste the papers on top of the blue grids on this page and the next two pages.

EQUIPMENT

pencils, markers   paste

special story

continues!

HOLD ON TIGHT
           Writer's Journal Magazine
      45

6

Finish your special story.

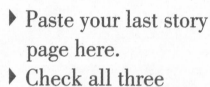

▶ Paste your last story page here.

▶ Check all three pages of your story.

▶ Are you happy with your story?

▶ Make changes if you want.

Your teacher will cut paper to cover the blue grid on this page.

Sharing information

Draw! Write! Paste!

▶ Draw pictures. Have the pictures tell about your information.

▶ Paste your pictures on the cut paper.

▶ Paste the cut paper on this page.

EQUIPMENT

pencils, markers   scissors

paste

old magazines or newspapers

8 Back cover

 Your teacher will cut paper to cover the blue grid on this page.

Your back cover

Make it!

▶ Draw pictures. Cut out pictures.

▶ Paste your pictures on the paper.

▶ Paste the cut paper to the blue grid on this page.

 pencils, markers

 scissors

 old magazines or newspapers

 paste